I GOT THE FLU! WHAT IS INFLUENZA?

Biology Book for Kids
Children's Diseases Books

BABY PROFESSOR

EDUCATION KIDS

Speedy Publishing LLC

40 E. Main St. #1156

Newark, DE 19711

www.speedypublishing.com

Copyright 2017

I feel yucky all over, like a big sickness monster is sitting on me! It's the flu! Read on and find out more about influenza and what to do about it.

WHAT IS THE FLU?

Influenza, or "the flu", is different from a common cold. A virus causes it, and it's an infectious disease. This means you can catch it from other people, especially if they cough or sneeze near you. The virus travels through the air on the cough or sneeze and can land on anybody nearby.

When you catch the flu it can make you so sick for a while that you can't go to school or work. And, of course, if you tried to go to school or a job, you might pass the flu on to other people. But most people with the flu just want to lie in bed.

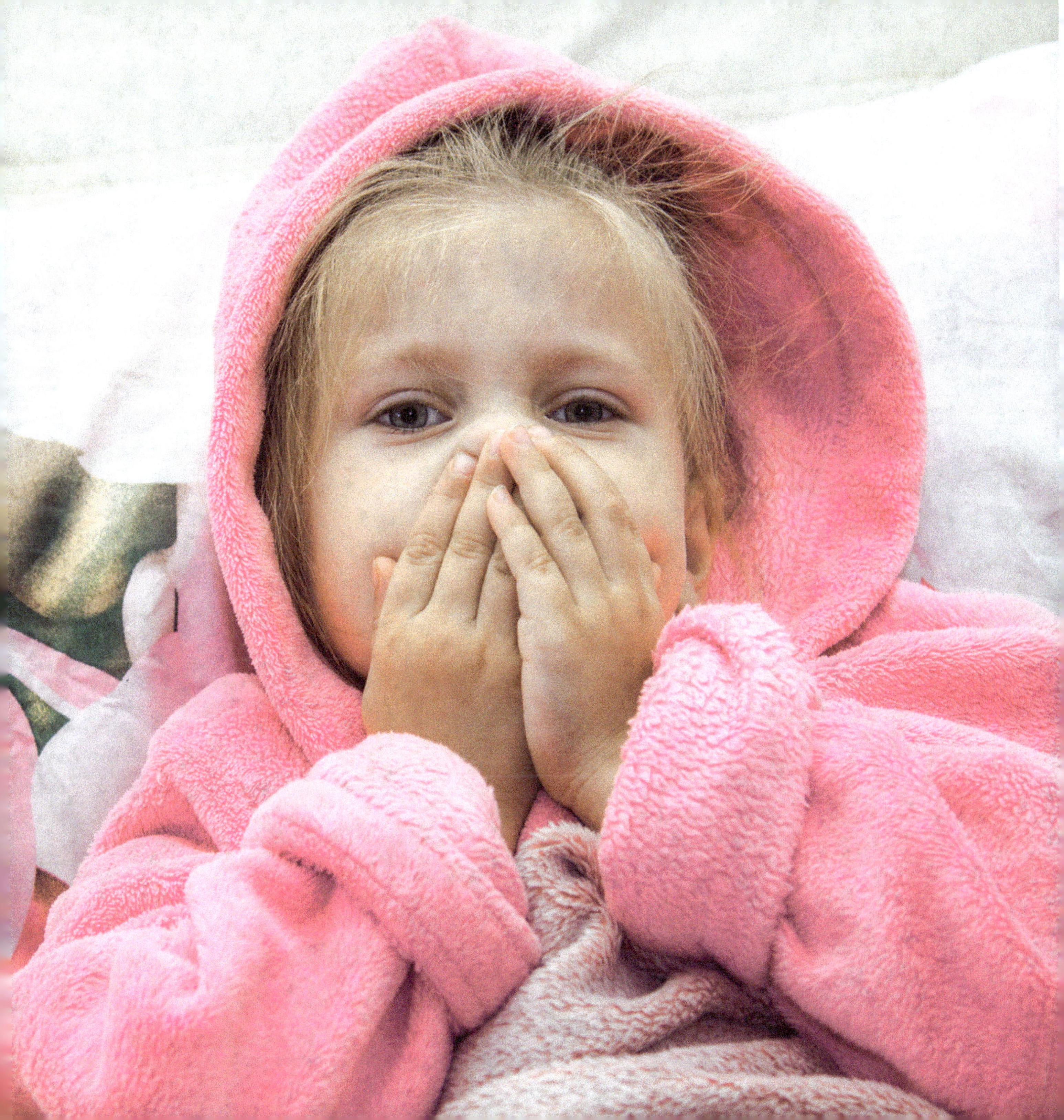

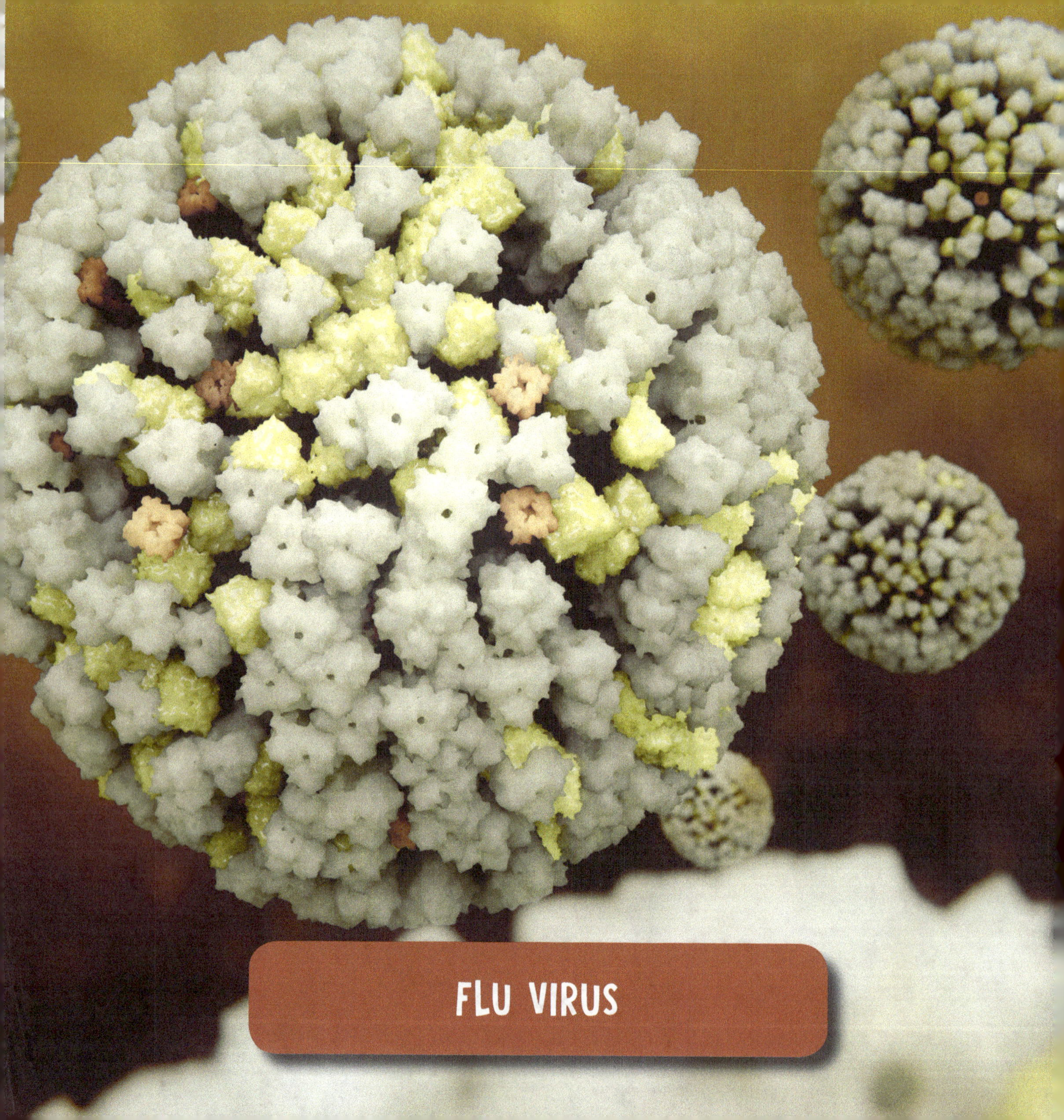
FLU VIRUS

If you get exposed to the flu virus, you may start feeling unwell a day or two later. But even before you feel sick yourself, you can accidentally pass the flu on to other people.

Once the flu settles in and you realize you have it, you are probably in for a week of feeling sick, possibly very sick. During this time you are still contagious, able to pass the flu on to others. You may get a cough on top of all sorts of other symptoms which we'll talk about in a minute, and the cough can stay with you for several weeks.

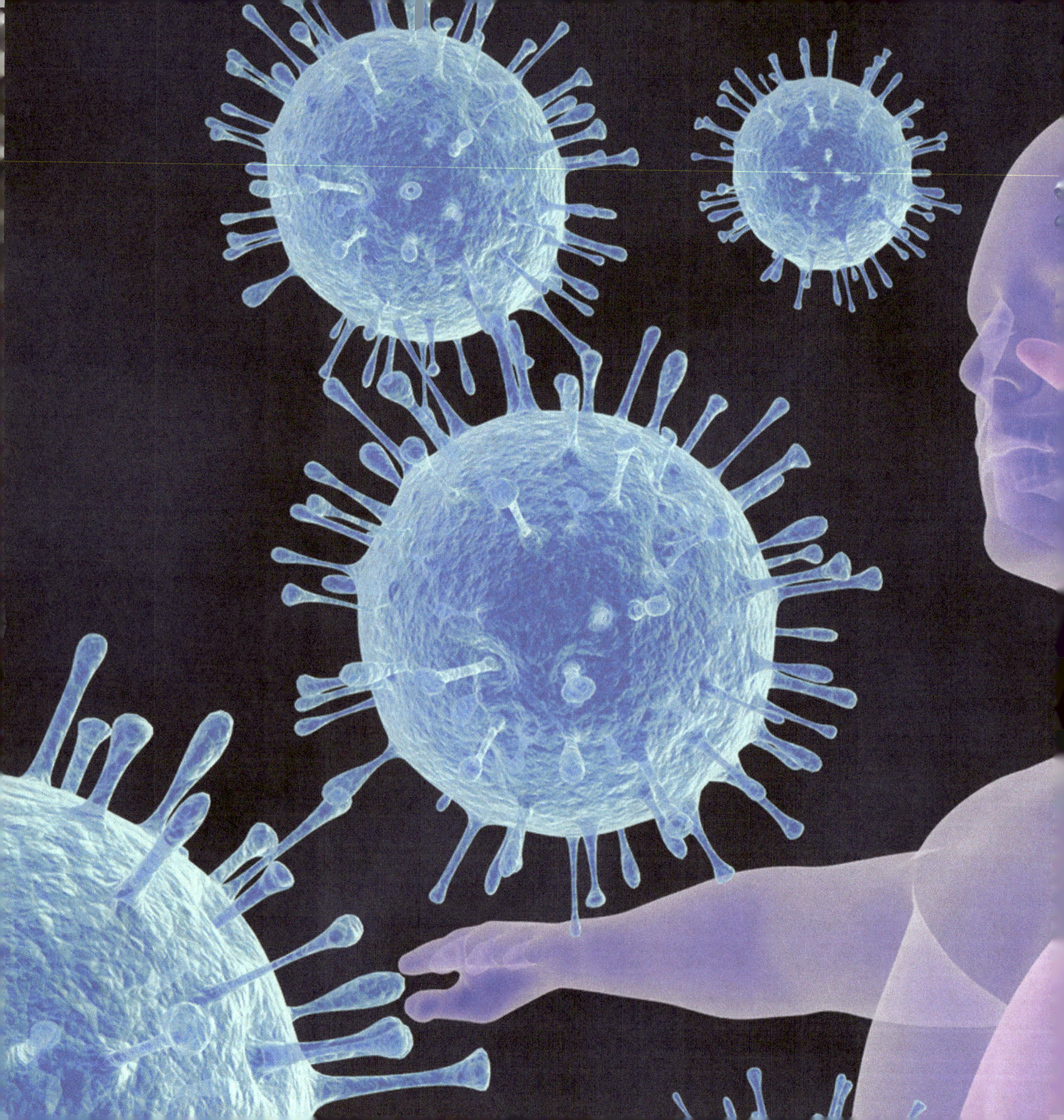

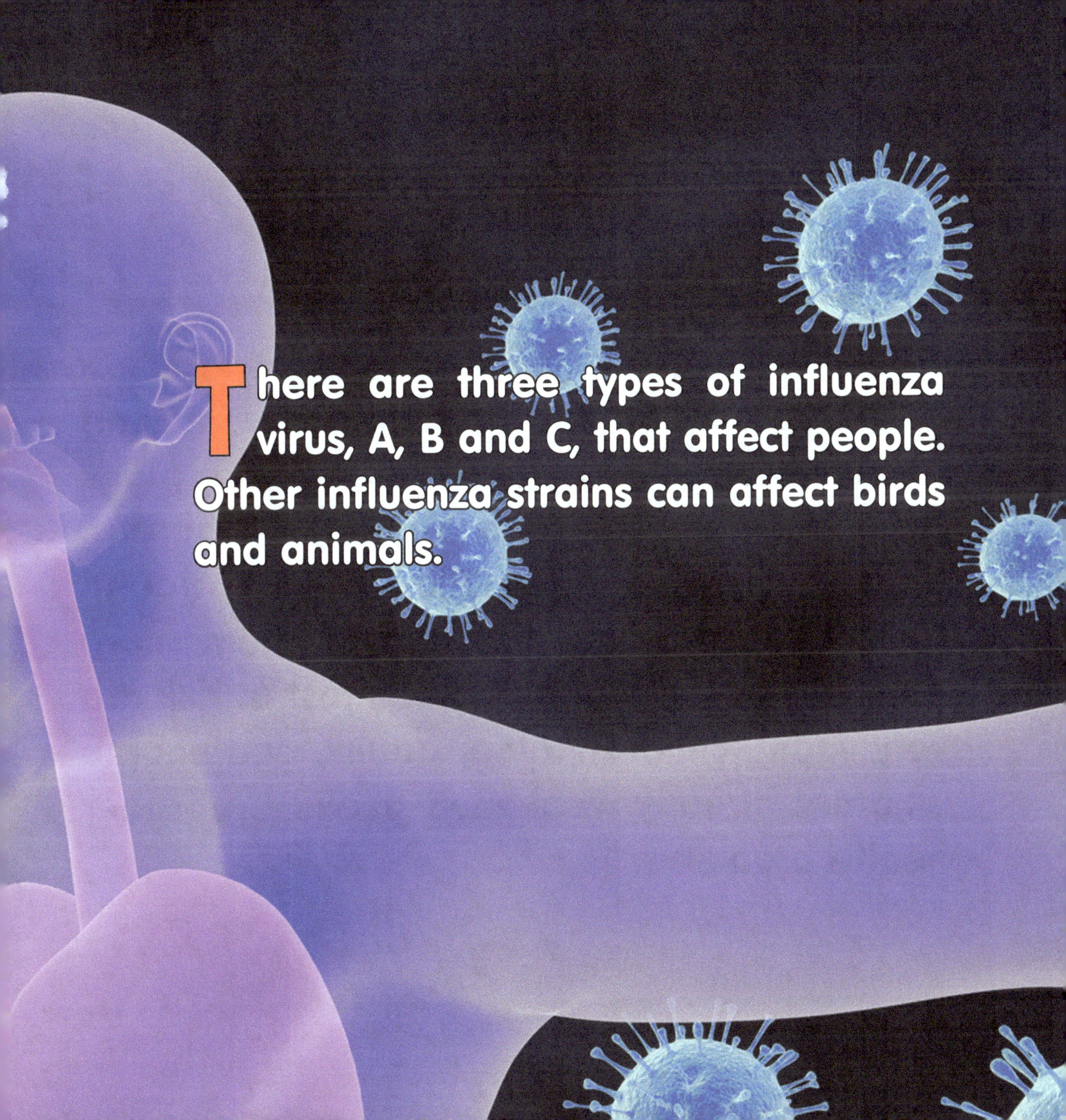

There are three types of influenza virus, A, B and C, that affect people. Other influenza strains can affect birds and animals.

THE FLU IS DANGEROUS

It's bad enough that catching the flu can make you feel lousy and mess up your plans for a week. But the flu is actually dangerous. Each year over three million people around the world catch the flu, and of them more than 250,000 die. The people most at risk are very young children, older adults, and people who are already weakened because of other health problems.

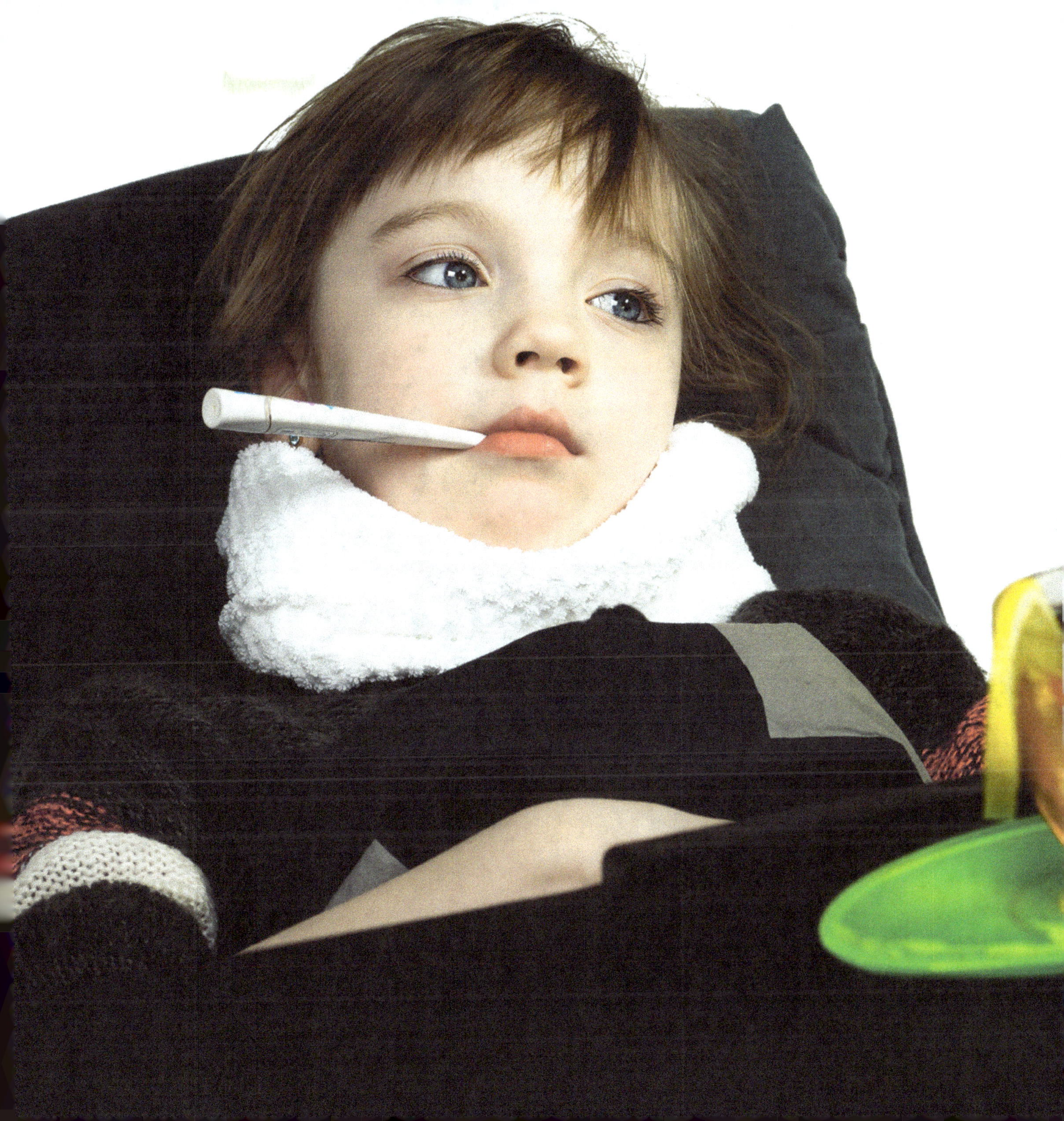

Around the Earth's equator, flu outbreaks can happen at any time of the year. Further north or south, such as in North America, Europe and Australia, influenza outbreaks usually happen in colder weather.

INFLUENZA OUTBREAK 1900s

EPIDEMICS

When a lot of people are getting sick, people call the outbreak an "epidemic", and local governments may declare a health emergency.

Since 1900 there have been a series of epidemics that were so large and so dangerous that people invented a new word for them: "pandemic". This meant that everybody seems to be getting the flu over a large part of the Earth.

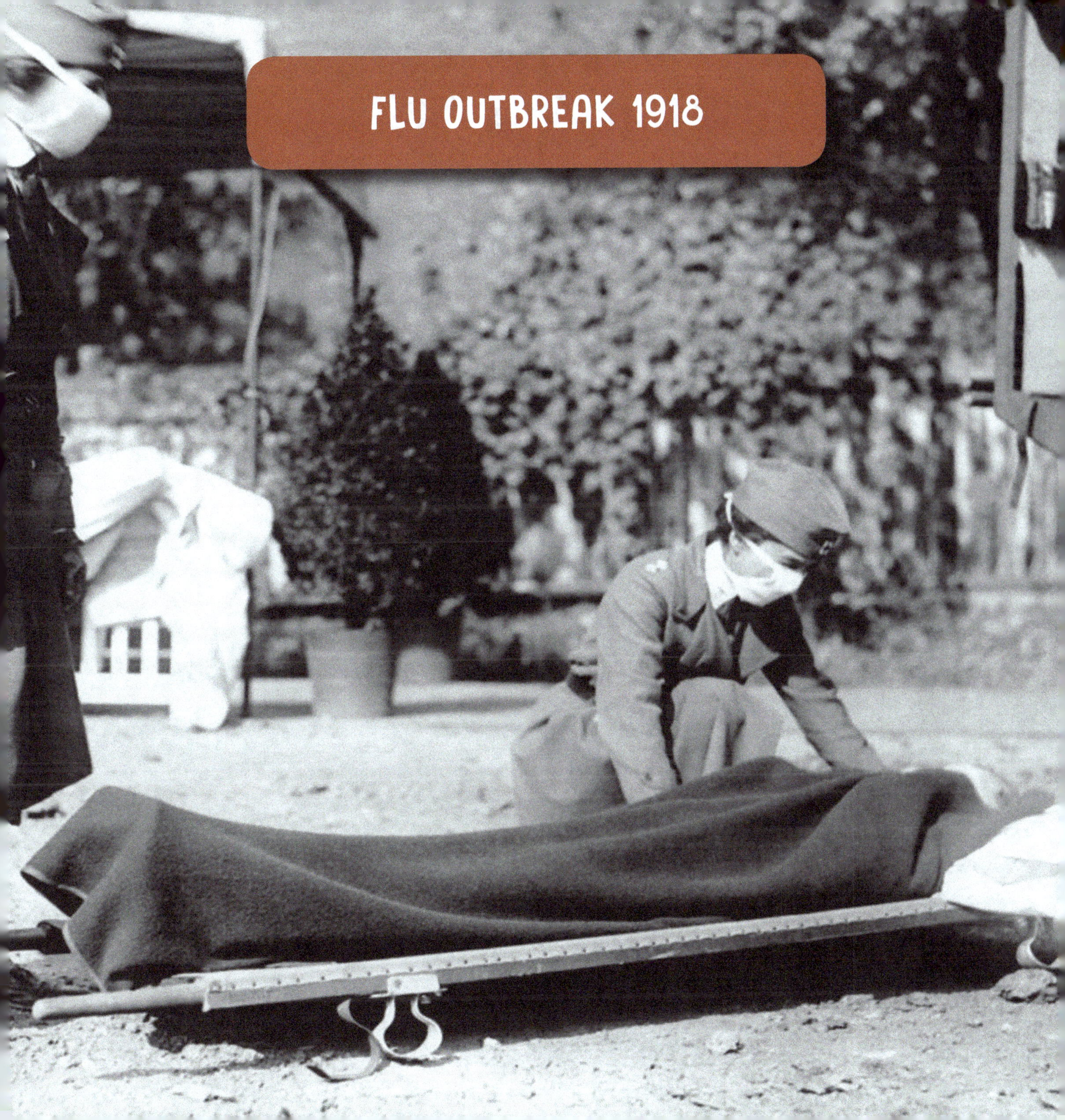

FLU OUTBREAK 1918

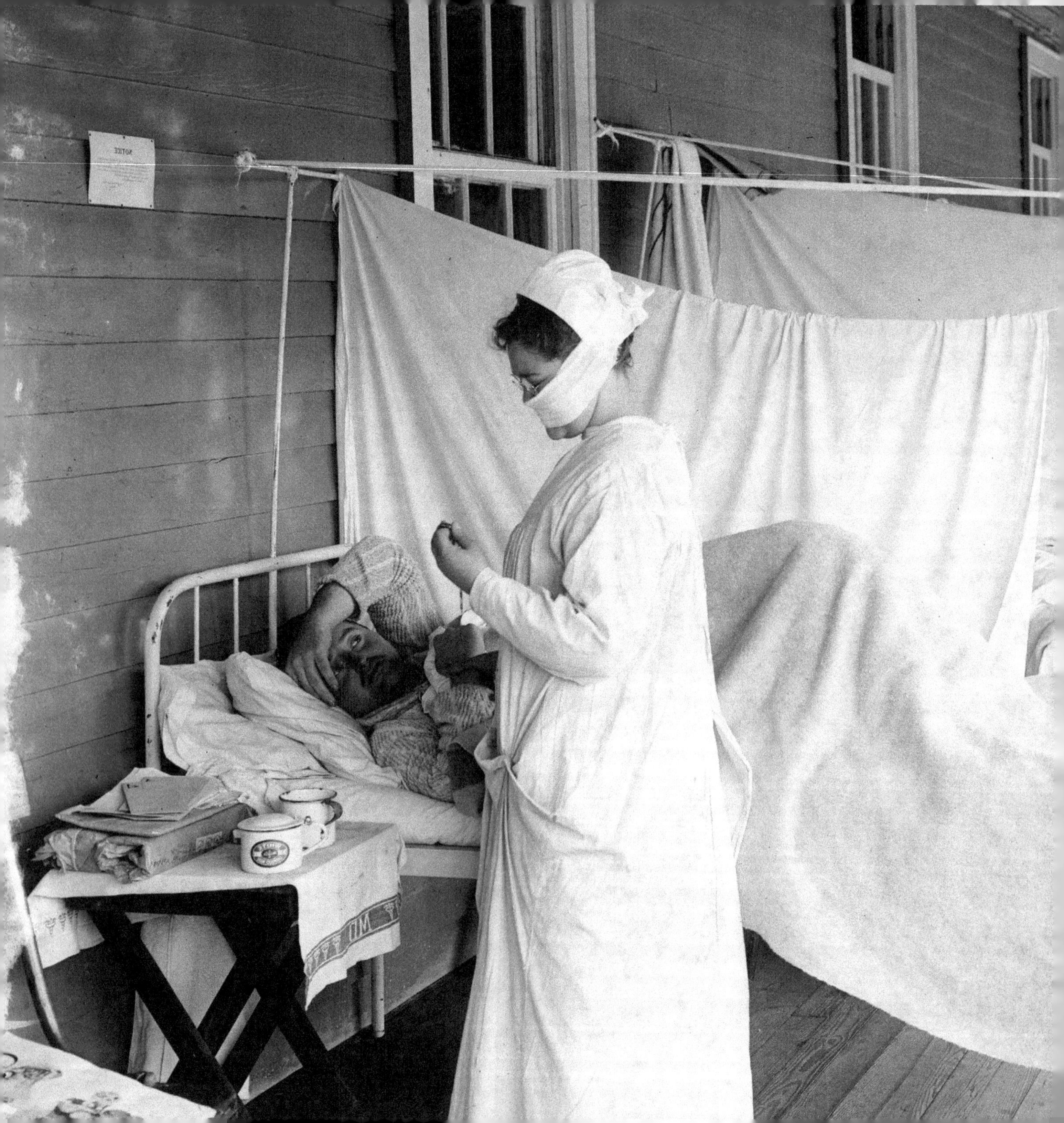

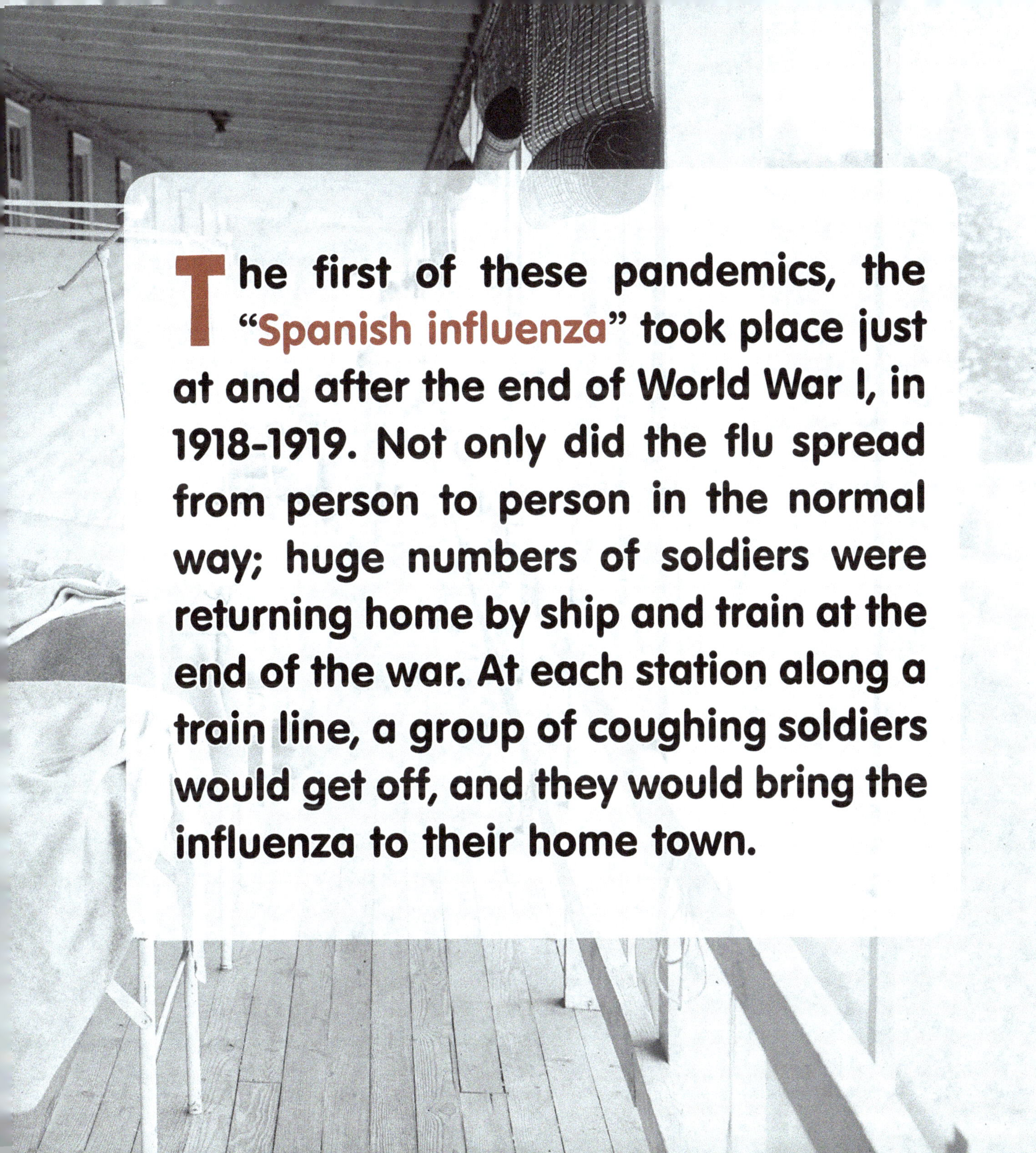

The first of these pandemics, the "Spanish influenza" took place just at and after the end of World War I, in 1918-1919. Not only did the flu spread from person to person in the normal way; huge numbers of soldiers were returning home by ship and train at the end of the war. At each station along a train line, a group of coughing soldiers would get off, and they would bring the influenza to their home town.

Over 500 million people became ill—about one in every three people on the whole planet—and between 20 and 30 million people died. This flu killed more people than the total number of people who died during World War I.

The Asian influenza in 1958 and the Hong Kong flu in 1968 each caused more than a million deaths.

LONG-TERM EFFECTS

When you have a cold you feel bad for a few days and your nose can get red and sore, and you use up a lot of tissues. But then you get better. People who catch the flu sometimes never get back to feeling the way they did before they got sick.

Most people who get the flu will completely recover in one or two weeks. Others, especially people whose systems are already weak for some other reason (including being very young or very old), may develop dangerous conditions like pneumonia.

The flu can cause complications for pregnant women and the children they are carrying, and for people who are recovering from heart transplants and similar major surgery. People with breathing problems like asthma and bronchitis, along with smokers, may have even more trouble getting enough air even after they are "recovered" from the flu.

People who are over fifty years old, and very young children, who get the flu are at a higher risk for other ailments like pneumonia, bronchitis, ear and sinus infections.

SYMPTOMS

How do you know you may have the flu? The most common symptoms, which may be quite severe, include a runny nose, a high fever followed by "chills" that make you shiver all over, and a sore throat. You may ache in all your muscles and have a headache that won't go away. You may develop a cough and feel like you want to go back to bed even if you just got up.

By the time you notice these symptoms, the influenza virus has already been in your body for a couple of days, and you may have been passing it on to others while you had no idea that you had caught the flu.

When people catch "stomach flu", or "the 24-hour flu", it's a different infectious disease that causes nausea and vomiting.

THESE ARE THE SYMPTOMS TO WATCH FOR:

- ➲ High fever followed by feeling extremely cold, with the fever coming back again
- ➲ A persistent cough
- ➲ Plugged-up and runny nose that you can't keep clear
- ➲ Sneezing
- ➲ Achy muscles and joints, and feeling crummy all over
- ➲ Feeling very tired

- A continuing headache
- Watery and itchy eyes
- Redness around the eyes, mouth, nose and throat
- Rashes on other parts of the body
- Small children may have stomach pain and diarrhea
- It's hard to tell the difference between a cold and the flu when it starts. High fever and feeling very tired are probably the strongest clues.

DON'T CATCH IT!

Nobody wants to catch the flu, so let's try to avoid it!

The most important thing you can do is to wash your hands several times a day with soap. Soap makes the flu virus inactive. This is a good daily habit to get into, not just in "flu season" but all around the year, because it can keep you safer from many kinds of infections.

ALWAYS WASH YOUR HANDS

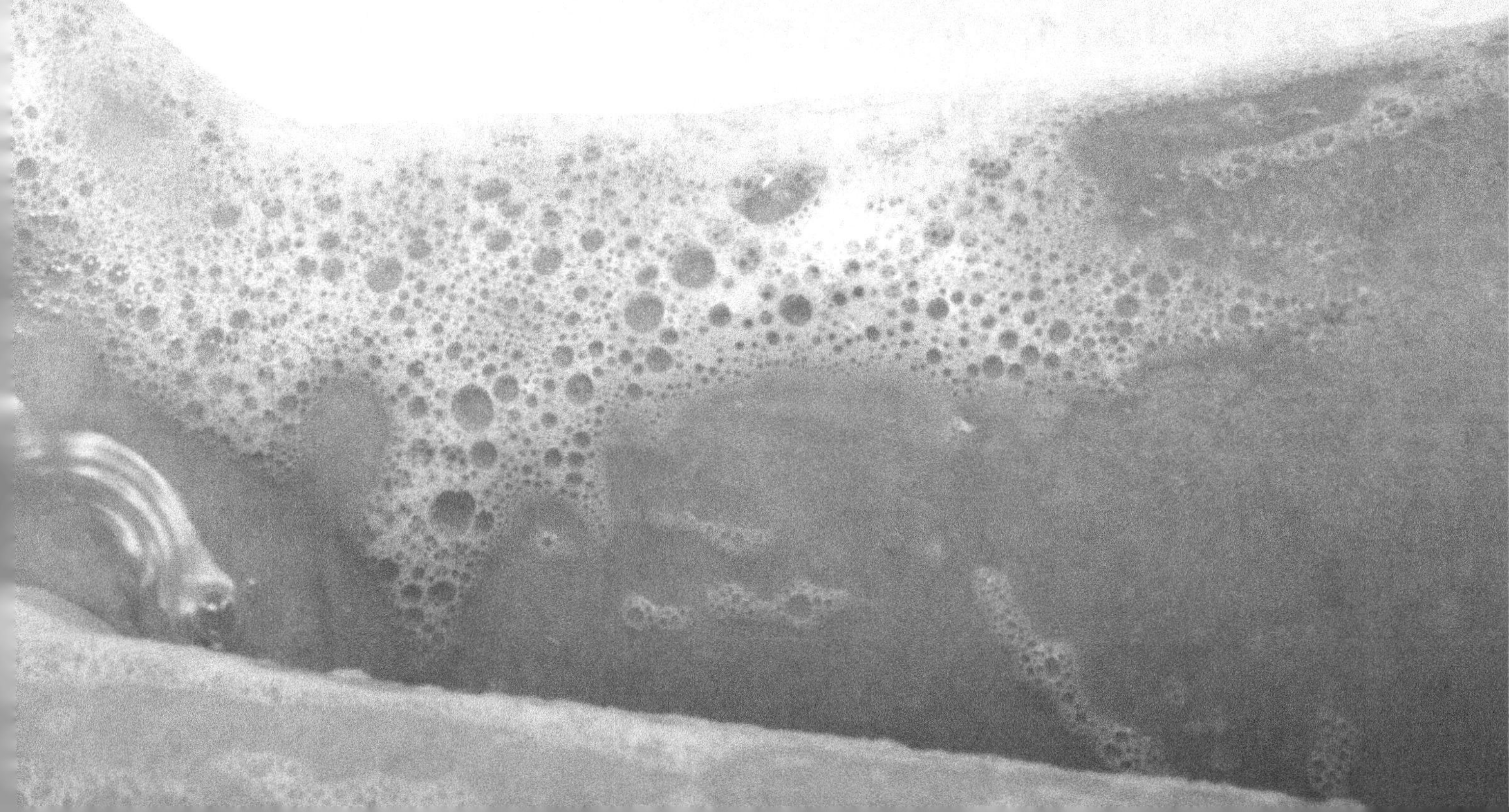

If you are out in public, shopping or playing, wash your hands with soap as soon as you get home. Try not to touch your fingers to your eyes or mouth before you have a chance to wash.

In many countries, like Japan, people wear masks over their mouths and noses during flu season, or if they have to travel a lot in crowded conditions like commuter trains. This cuts down on them passing along the flu, as well as catching it from others.

JAPANESE LADY WEARING A MASK

FLU SHOT

In many countries health services offer a flu shot before and during "flu season". The shot is developed each year based on doctors' and scientists' best estimate of which strains of influenza (A, B, C, a combination of them, or something new) are going to cause the most trouble in the coming months. A flu shot that is effective in one year may not be very useful in the next year, because the influenza virus keeps evolving.

Many countries offer this shot for free, or for very little, because the cost of preventing flu is much less than the cost of lost work days and medical care for people who fall ill.

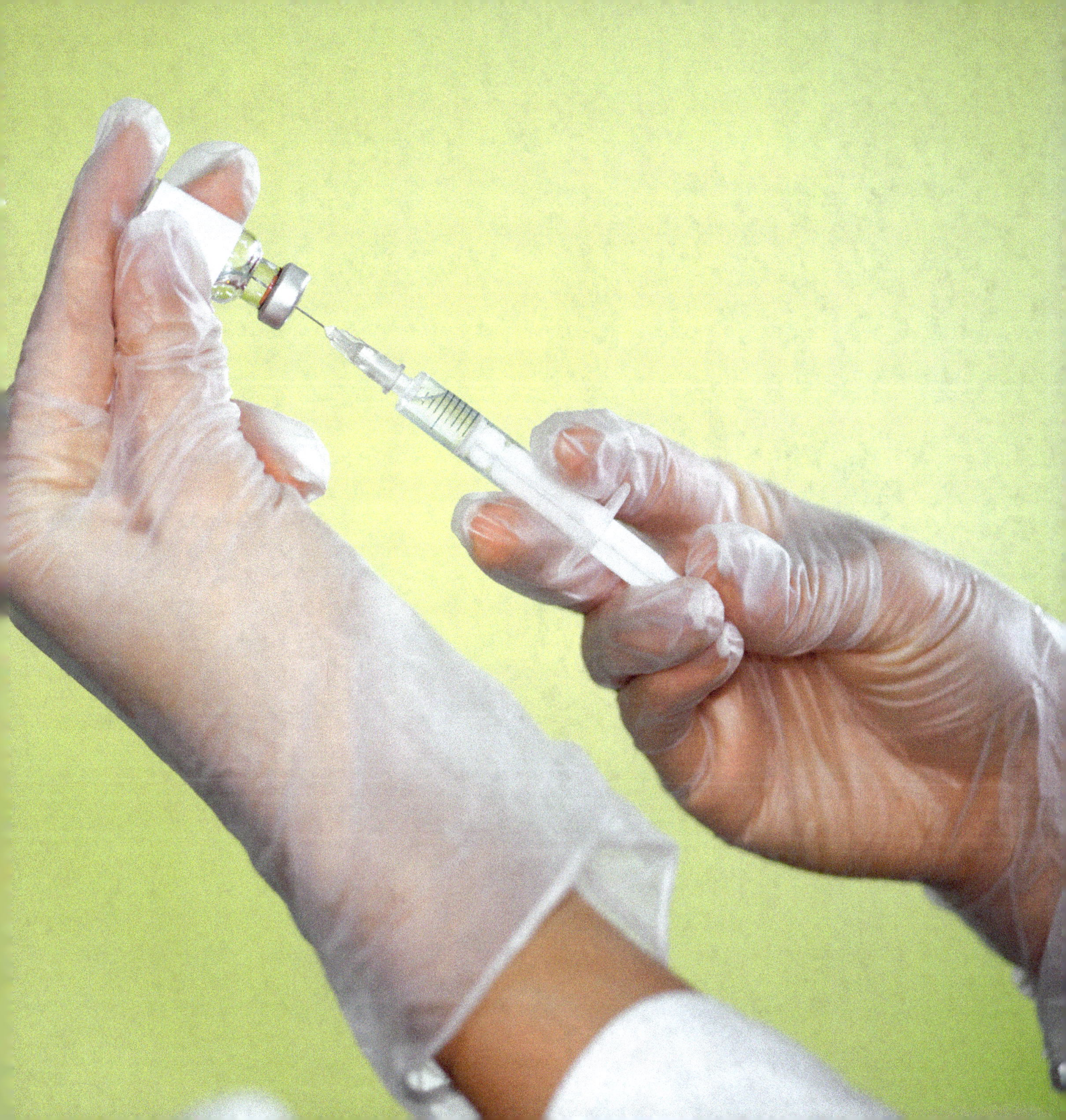

The flu shot is highly recommended for small children, pregnant women, people over 50 years old, and people who already have trouble breathing because of some existing condition.

HOW TO GET BETTER

If you realize you have the flu soon after you become infected, and your doctor agrees, the doctor may give you an antiviral drug. These drugs work well if given soon after the person becomes infected, but are less useful once the flu has really taken hold and you are huddling in bed just wishing the whole world would go away.

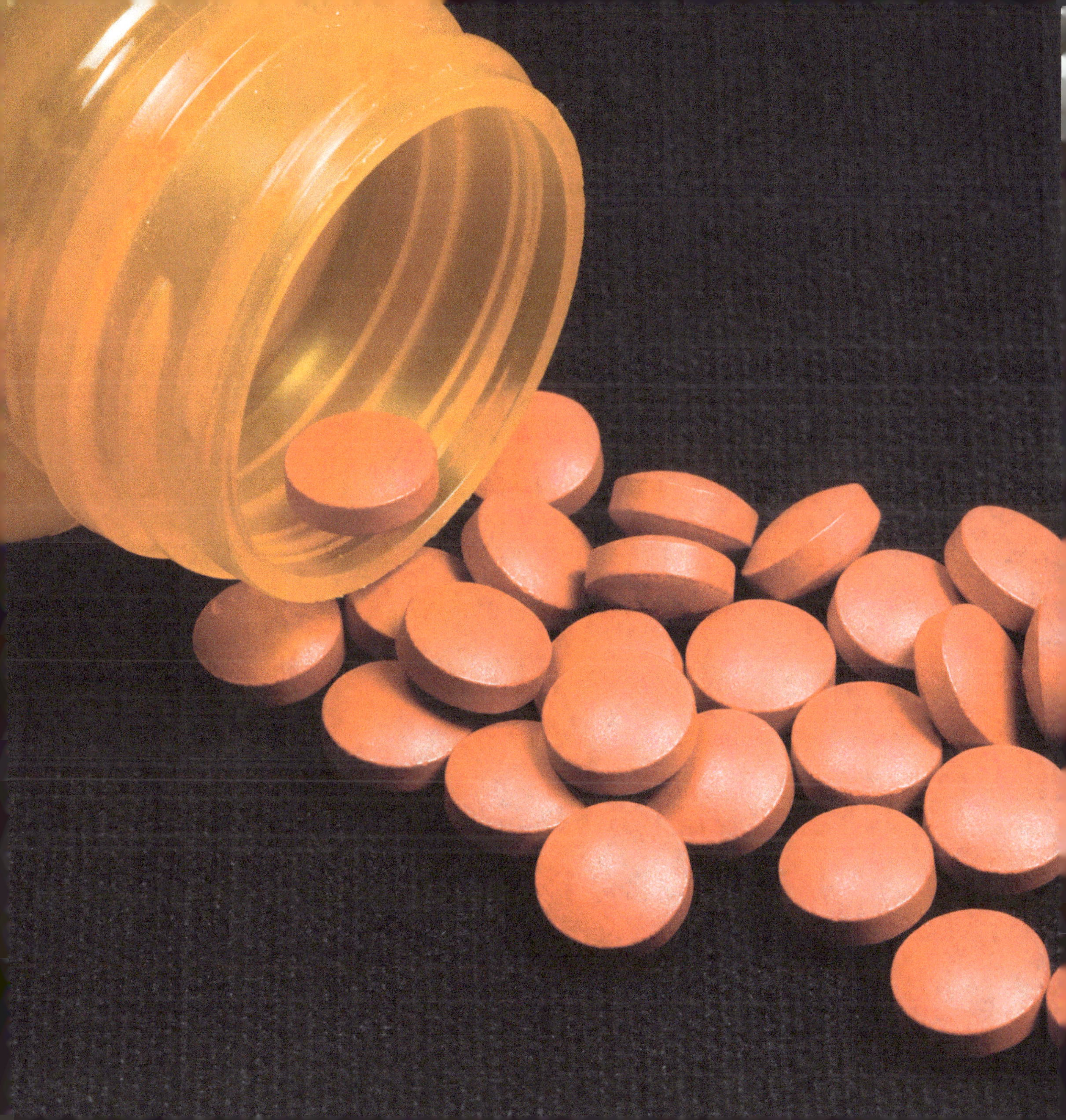

Once you have the flu, the main things that will help, and at least help you be more comfortable, are getting lots of rest and drinking plenty of fluids like water and tea. Avoid sugary drinks and anything with alcohol in it.

For aches and pains, and to reduce your fever, you can take pain relievers like acetaminophen. Children and teenagers who have the flu should avoid taking aspirin, especially if they have caught influenza type B, to avoid damaging their livers.

Since a virus causes influenza, antibiotics have no effect on it. However, antibiotics are helpful if the person develops pneumonia or some other secondary condition while weakened with the flu.

The other important point is to avoid infecting other people. You don't want to give to others what is causing you to feel bad! Cover your mouth when coughing and sneezing, don't go out in public if you don't have to, and concentrate on getting better.

GET HEALTHY AND STAY HEALTHY

Your good health makes it possible to lead a good life! Read other Baby Professor books, like The Top 50 Quick Facts about the Human Body, to learn more about your body and your health.

Visit
BABY PROFESSOR
EDUCATION KIDS
www.BabyProfessorBooks.com
to download Free Baby Professor eBooks
and view our catalog of new and exciting
Children's Books